Managers, fin

u~~sers.~~

While your colleagues are constantly struggling to create Excel reports and meet impossible deadlines,

You can overtake them, reaching a high level of expertise even if you have no prior experience in programming!
I invite you to learn the ACM method, and become 'Masters' of Excel VBA!

ACM

Advanced studies in everyday language,
easily understood by people who are not programmers!

Today it is obvious that, with the knowledge contained in EXCEL VBA, you will be far ahead of the crowd! Nonetheless, many people still believe that only programmers can learn Excel VBA programming.

That's not true !

Using the unique method personally developed by me - integrating knowledge obtained from many years' experience in programming and teaching - will make you an expert in Excel VBA.

Even with no prior programming experience, in a brief time you will gain a reputation for professionalism, and will take the lead ahead of your bosses and colleagues!
The method has been tested on large numbers of students for over 15 years, and has changed the lives of thousands of managers, financiers and other Excel users.

> ## "Totally Worth the money"
>
> Robert E. White, Orlandom FL

Step by step, my book will reveal to you how you, too, can achieve a level of expertise without prior knowledge of programming. 'translating' programming language into everyday language and using as little terminology/professional jargon as possible, you, too, can become a expert in EXCEL VBA.

> ## Saved me hours of work.
> ## Thank you!
>
> Raymond Betts, Stamford, CT

I'll reveal all the secrets:

- You will learn the main syntax of the language, step by step.
- You will benefit from the capabilities of Excel, which will save time while streamlining operations.
- You will receive simple, easily understood instructions.
- You will upgrade your professional capability in Excel.
- You will start developing your own software to manage advanced information – not possible without VBA language.
- You will surprise colleagues and bosses... and especially yourself!
- Everything with a click of a button and in a fraction of the time - with a proven method that has already accelerated thousands of managers to a new level of knowledge !

You have no idea how much I appreciate you and how grateful I am to you, even without knowing you personally, so I'll simply say "Thank you very very much!"

Susie Albright, New York, NY

I wish you a pleasant learning experience

Maayan Poleg

Abstract

Microsoft Excel has, over the years, become the greatest software in the field of electronic worksheets.

Its strength is that it meets the demands of huge numbers of users worldwide. Nonetheless - despite the advancement and expanding use of this software - there is ever-increasing demand from the end users; much of which can only be solved by VBA programming (**V**isual **B**asic for **A**pplications).

Therefore, "**Excel VBA – In Everyday Language**" was written in order to provide a response to the growing demand for the advanced capabilities of Microsoft Excel.

This book was written:

- For the "non-programmers" among us who have to create the same reports in Microsoft Excel time and again, and would like to automate the process.

- For people who wish to develop forms, screens and "machines" for data management within their organization.

- For individuals who wish to turn Microsoft Excel into a powerful tool in their daily work.

During the writing process I tried to visualize Microsoft Excel software and the VB editor through the eyes of the end users; people who may not have programming background, but aspire to reap the utmost from the program.

For this reason the book, based on many years' of experience in programming and training, has been written in everyday language, using as few technical terms as possible, to make for easy reading.

My goal, when writing this book, was to convey the main principles of VBA language and allow beginners, taking their first steps, to learn without requiring individual training.

For this purpose there are files of exercises accompanying the book. These may be downloaded from bit.ly/Excel-VBA.

The exercise files are in .xls format, allowing the end users to use either the "Ribbon Versions" (2007 and higher) or other older versions of Microsoft Excel.

This new edition has undergone extensive processing and addresses Microsoft Excel 2010/2013 users, along with explanations for anyone using the older versions (2003 and 2007). Therefore, wherever there is a significant difference between Excel 2010/2013 and the old versions, explanations are provided in full.

I wish you a pleasant entry into the world of VBA!

Maayan Poleg

Table of Contents

Warning

This book was written specifically for Microsoft Excel users who want to expand their knowledge of this software.

Considerable effort has been invested to write a book that is as complete and reliable as possible, although that does not imply any guarantee.

The author is not responsible for any loss or damage which may be caused to any individual or organization, if any, due to the information contained in this book.

It is highly recommended to back-up all work data prior to executing any changes.

Introduction

VBA is a programming language designed for use with a variety of Microsoft Office software. This language allows the basic options inherent in the software to be expanded. Thus, the user gets the utmost benefit by the creation of tailor-made applications.

This book focuses on the VBA language for Microsoft Excel.

Why you should become familiar with VBA language?

There are two main reasons:

Firstly, it is possible to utilize a macro to automate frequently repeated processes.

Secondly, the VBA programming language enables the user to add features that are not directly supported by Microsoft Excel, such as:

- Providing user alerts and notifications
- Receiving data from user
- Performing loops on data
- Creating forms
- And much more...

By writing VBA codes you can enrich Microsoft Excel files, turning them into powerful tools for your personal needs, or for the needs of your organization.

Reading guidelines

For readability and practice, you should become familiar with the semantics used in the writing of this book:

- When the names of two keys appear with the sign "+" between them, you should press on both keys simultaneously. For example – to open the VB editor you must press on the keyboard shortcut **Alt+F11** (in other words, hold down the Alt key when pressing F11).

- Tips, comments and programming codes will appear in a gray box.

For example:

```
Sub FontSize()
 ActiveCell.Font.Size = 14
End Sub
```

- Practical exercises will appear in a numbered list

For example:

```
1. Open the VB editor
2. Add A module
```

- The sub-menus selection from the Main Menu will appear with the sign "->" to indicate the order of operations.

For example:

Select '**Tools**' -> '**Macro**' -> '**Macros**'

- Although there is no need to add blank lines between the different parts of the code, they were added to make reading easier, and to clarify matters for beginners.

Basic Terms

This chapter contains a list of basic terms.

These terms will be clarified during the learning process and practice.

VBA	An event-oriented language that relates to objects.
Macro/Code	Sequence of actions that enables process automation (macros can be recorded or written manually).
Objects	"Building Blocks" of the program – workbook, worksheet, range, column, row etc., On objects you can perform actions such as calculation, design, copying, etc.
Collections	Grouping objects of the same type, for example – collection of worksheets or charts.
Object Properties	Each object has properties. Background, for example, is a property of a range.

Method	Actions on objects, for example - you can run a method (action) of a copy on a range-type object.
Event	Each action takes place on a worksheet, such as - clicking, selecting etc.
Module	Component of the VB editor which can store code lines in it.
Absolute Macro	A Macro that operates on a pre-set range, regardless of the current location in the worksheet.
Relative Macro	A Macro that operates on ranges in accordance with the current location in the worksheet.
Routine	Sequence of actions to perform.
Variable	Memory "stack" designed to store temporary values while the code is running.

Developer Tab

Starting from the Microsoft Excel 2007 version, the user interface has changed significantly, and now displays 'ribbons' instead of toolbars. Therefore, Excel 2007-2013 will, from now on, be called the "ribbon versions".

In these versions the different actions related to macro and code writing appear in the '**Developer**' tab.

The tab does not appear as a default, and must be added manually.

Add Developer Tab to Microsoft Excel 2010/2013 version

1. Click the **File** tab

2. Click **Options**

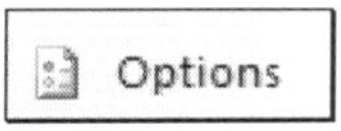

3. Click **Customize Ribbon**.

4. In **Customize the Ribbon,** under **Main Tabs**, select **Developer**, as shown in the following image:

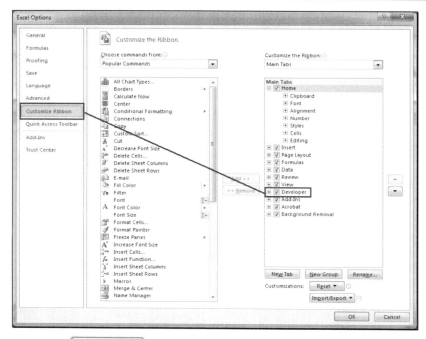

5. Click OK .
6. The **Developer** tab will appear:

Add Developer Tab to Microsoft Excel 2007 version

1. Click the Office button to open the menu.
2. Click Excel Options
3. Under **Popular**, select **'Show Developer tab in the Ribbon'** .

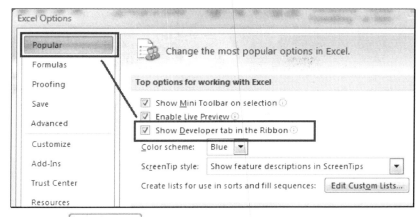

4. Click OK.

5. The **Developer** tab will appear:

Security

Microsoft Office 2007 version was the first to introduce the '**Trust Center**', where you can change the security settings for Office files.

Trusted Locations

Trusted Location is a folder that enables the files saved in it to be opened without being checked by the Trust Center's security features. Make sure to save only files from a reliable origin in this folder.

Trusted Locations Settings for Microsoft Excel 2010/2013 version

1. Click **File** to open the menu.

2. Click. **Options**

3. Under **Trust Center**, click **Trust Center Settings**, as shown in the following image:

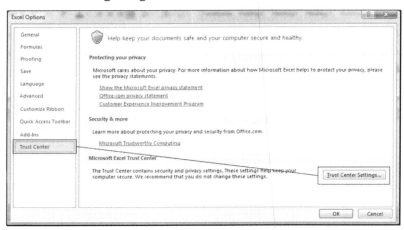

4. The following window will open:

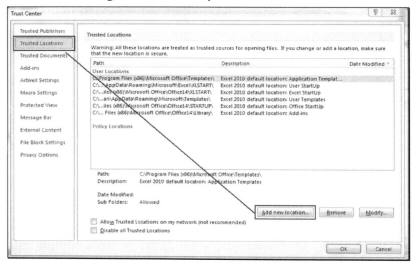

5. Under **Trusted Locations** click **Add new location**.

6. The following window will open:

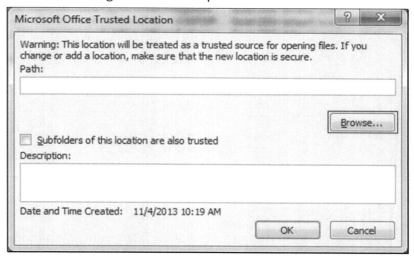

7. Click Browse to select the desired folder, and then click

OK .

You can set the subfolder in the location to also be considered as 'trusted'.

8. The folder will be added to the trusted locations list. Files with macro commands in the folder will be activated without notification.

Remove a Trusted Location

In the Trusted Locations window, as shown in section 4 above, select the location you wish to remove from the trusted locations list and click Remove .

Trusted Locations Settings for Microsoft Excel 2007 version

1. Click the Office button to open the menu.

2. Click Excel Options

3. Under **Trust Center** click **Trust Center Settings**, as shown in the following image:

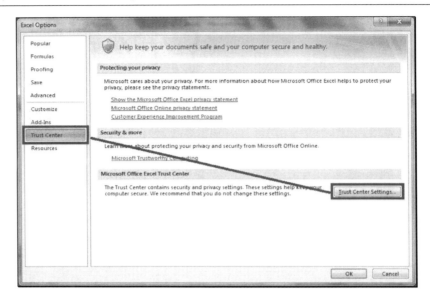

4. The following window will open:

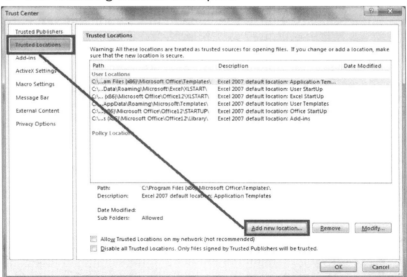

5. Under **Trusted Locations** click **Add new location**.

6. The following window will open:

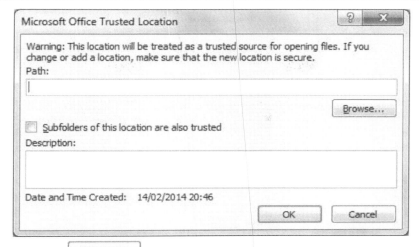

7. Click [Browse...] to select the desired folder and then click [OK]. You can set the subfolder in this location to also be considered as trusted.

8. The folder will be added to the 'Trusted Locations' list. Files with macro commands in the folder will be activated without notification.

Remove a Trusted Location

In the trusted locations window, as shown in section 4 above, click the trusted location that you want to remove from the trusted locations list and click [Remove].

Security Level

In addition to trusted locations there are general security options that apply to files outside a trusted folder.

In order to run macros on those files, the security level should be lowered.

Macro Security Settings for the Ribbon Versions

1. On the **Developer** tab, in the **Code** group, click

2. The following window will open:

3. Select the desired security level.

Macro Security Settings for Microsoft Excel 2003

1. Select **Tools -> Macro -> Security**.

2. Select the desired security level.

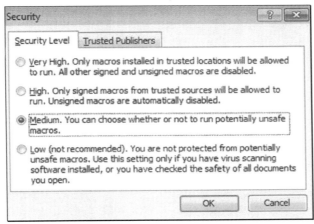

3. Click ` OK `

Saving Files

Until the Microsoft Excel 2003 version, files were saved with an ".xls" extension.

In the 'Ribbon versions' the extension of the Excel workbook was changed to ".xlsx".

This file extension does not allow macro commands that were recorded or written in it to be saved.

In order to enable the workbook to save the macros, it should be saved with the extension ".xlsm".

Note:

When trying to save an Excel file that contains macros with the extension ".xlsx", the following warning will appear:

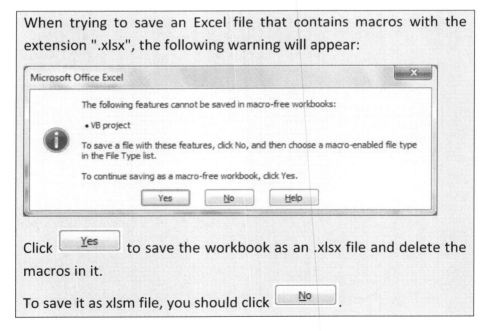

Click [Yes] to save the workbook as an .xlsx file and delete the macros in it.

To save it as xlsm file, you should click [No].

Important to Know:

Saving the file with the .xls extension will allow running macros in the Ribbon versions as well, but will limit the number of rows and columns in the workbook, in accordance with the number in Excel 2003.

(In the Excel 2003 version the number of rows is 65,536; whereas in the ribbon versions the number of rows is 1,048,576).

Visual Basic Editor - VBE

Enter VB Editor

For the 'Ribbon Versions'

On the **Developer** tab, click
Or click the shortcut **Alt+F11** on the keyboard.

For Microsoft Excel 2003

Select **Tools -> Macro -> Visual Basic Editor**
Or click the shortcut **Alt+F11** on the keyboard.

If you add the VBA toolbar ![toolbar] to the toolbar menu you will be able to enter the VB editor by clicking the icon ![icon].

VB Editor

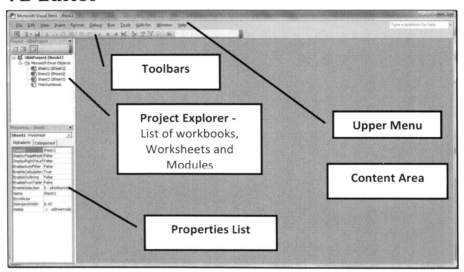

Please note that, by default, the VB editor opens without modules.
Add a module by selecting **Insert -> Module** (you cannot write in the
gray content area if the module has not been added).

The module will be added to the list in the **Project** window.

Note:

> The VB editor might open differently in your computer than it appears
> in the image above. Later in this chapter you will learn how to adjust
> the display of the window so that it appears similar to the example
> above.

The Structure of the VB Editor

The VB editor window is divided into several areas:

- **Menu** – contains menus such as File, Edit, etc.

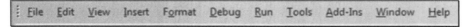

- **Toolbars** – contains the most useful commands from the menus.

- **Content Area** – here you can write, edit and activate the codes. Most activities in the content area will be conducted in **Modules**.
- **Explorer** - Displays the list of projects, workbooks, worksheets and modules. If the window does not appear, click on the menu **View -> Project Explorer**, or press the key combination **Ctrl+R.**
- To display the codes, double-click on the desired workbook, worksheet or module, from the explorer window.

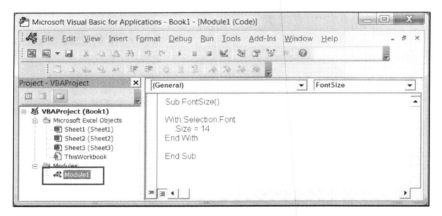

- If you have opened a number of workbooks, note which workbook you are writing the code in, because this is the workbook the macro will be saved in (you can check that you are actually writing in the correct workbook using **Project Explorer**).
- There is no significance to the module in which the codes are written, as long as they are written in the correct workbook.
- Every time you open Microsoft Excel and record a macro, it is recorded in a new module.
- As long as the file is open, all codes are recorded in the same module.

- The location of the recorded macro cannot be controlled, but you can move the codes from one module to another after recording; this is done by using 'cut and paste'.

Adapting the VB Editor Workspace

You can change The VB editor workspace by selecting **Tools** → **Options**.

Editor Tab

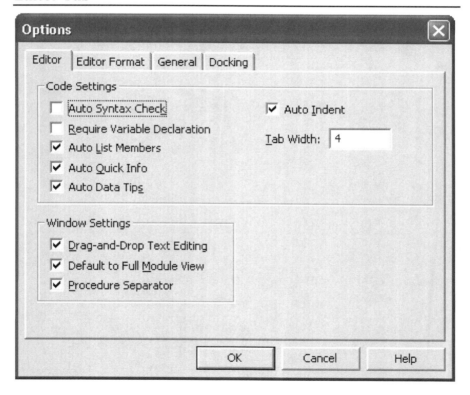

Auto Syntax Check	Determines whether an alert will appear whenever a syntax error is detected. If you don't want these alerts to appear, uncheck (remove the √ sign) the check box (incorrect syntax is highlighted in red).
Require Variable Declaration	Requires the user to declare variables comprehensively. Note - If you want to make the user declare variables in a specific module only, you can use the **Option Explicit** command at the top of the module (details of the 'declaration of variables' on page 73).
Auto List Members	Offers help when typing the command by showing the list of properties belonging to it (see page 58).
Auto Quick Info	Displays the required arguments while typing a command.
Auto Data Tips	When you place the cursor on it, it displays the variable value while the macro is running.

Editor Format Tab

Allows you to set the font formats (type and size) for the codes, comments, breakpoints, etc...

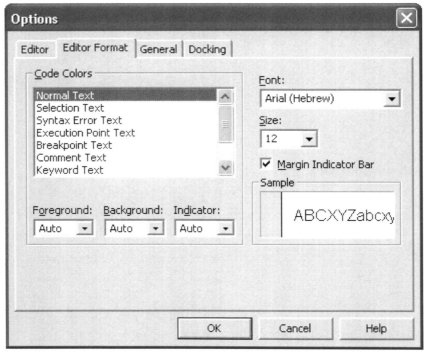

In order to select the design, highlight the desired option.

Normal Text changes the text color used for writing code.

Selection Text is used to change the selected text color.

Execution Point Text is used to change the color of the next line executed.

Note:

You can see the settings preview in the sample window.

General Tab

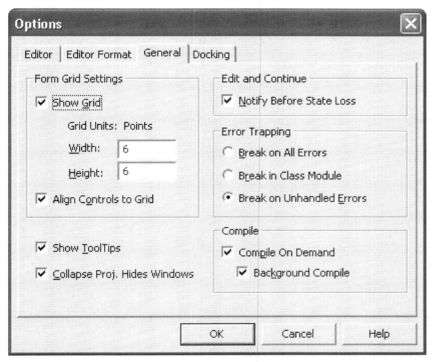

The tab is divided into several areas:

Form Grid Settings:

Refers to the grid lines when designing forms.

Edit and Continue:

Allows to determine whether a warning message will be displayed; warning that specific actions will reset variables

Error Trapping:

Allows a choice between different options to stop running the code when an error occurs.

Docking Tab

Allows determining which of the windows will be fixed to the screen and which will "float".

When a window is fixed to the screen you can attach it to one side of the editor (usually the bottom or side of the window)

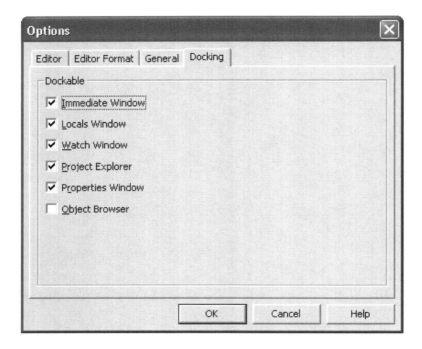

FROM OUR FAMILY TO YOURS.....

MERRY CHRISTMAS

"What if Christmas, he
thought, doesn't come from
a store. What if Christmas,
perhaps, means a little bit
more."
- Dr. Seuss

THE VRBAS CLAN

CHRIS, AURORA, & AMANDA

A Moment Before We Start...

Code writing can be simple, if you follow a few basic rules.

It is not random that a VBA file is called a "Project" – it is absolutely a project and, as with every project, proper planning and strict working rules will allow for smooth and efficient implementation later on. Or, as the wise men said: "Think before you act".

So, before sitting down to record a macro or write a code, read the following instructions:

- **Create a backup copy**: before you start writing a code, create a backup copy of the original workbook so you can recover data if necessary.

- **Definition of project goals**: ahead of time, define the purpose of the code and the desired final product. Such definition will enable you to evaluate the development time required, as well as the necessary resources for implementation.

- **Decomposition of a project into its components**: Which tasks in the code must be developed in order to produce the final pre-defined product?

- **Writing the code**: This is the practical part of writing a macro (VBA code). The main contents of this book focus on "How to write what you need".

- **Leave time for testing**: Allow yourself the right to be wrong. There was never a programmer who wrote a code that "ran at the first shot"; after you finish reading this book, you will not be exempt from testing. Be prepared that something in the code will not work the first time. That's to be expected, because it happens to everyone ...

- **Write Comments**: There is nothing more annoying than going back to a code you wrote a year ago and trying to figure it out...

- **Don't know how to write? Record!** Many times you will discover that you don't know how to write a specific code command. Our advice is to record it. Then view the code and learn the relevant commands.

- **There is nothing like F1**: Get into the habit of using the VBA help. Often you will discover that the nuances of the commands can change their outcome. Placing the cursor on a command and pressing F1 on the keyboard will display relevant explanations for that command, as well as options and further examples.

- **Do not re-invent the wheel**: Check the web, do research, consult forums and ask questions. Efficient searching can save you many hours of work that someone else has already done!

Objects

The way in which the VB Editor communicates with Microsoft Excel is by referring to objects.

Objects, for example, are: the application itself (Microsoft Excel software), a workbook, a worksheet, a row, a column, a chart and so on.

The objects have:

- **Properties** – for example: font color is a property of the object 'Font'.
- **Methods** – for example: copying is a method (action) that can be Performed on a 'Range' object.
- **Events** – for example: selecting a cell or changing a value are events that can activate a macro.
- **Related Objects** – for example: there are objects related to the worksheet objects, such as rows, columns, etc.

The objects are arranged hierarchically, with the main object being the Microsoft Excel software itself, which enables actions at the software level. Reference is made to it using the **Application** command.

Note:

The explanations for writing commands will appear in the chapter on page 53

Please note that in some cases you can omit the name of the "parent object", for example: the command to add a worksheet.

Application.Worksheets.Add

Can also be written in an abbreviated version:

Worksheets.Add

But, the command:

```
Range("A1").Name = "FirstCell"
```

Is significantly different from the command:

```
Worksheets("Sheet1").Range("A1").Name = "FirstCell"
```

This is due to the fact that the first code applies the name "FirstCell" to cell A1 in the active worksheet, while the second code applies the name FirstCell to cell A1 in "Sheet 1", regardless of the worksheet from which we run the code.

Macro Recording

The basic way to automate processes is by recording a macro directly from the Microsoft Excel software:

Display 'Record Macro' Window in the 'Ribbon versions'

Click on 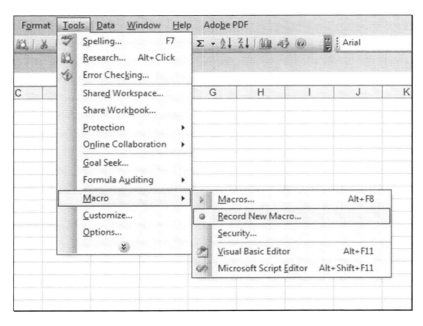 in the **Developer** tab.

Display 'Record Macro' Window in Excel 2003 version

Select **Tools** → **Macro** → **Record New Macro**...:

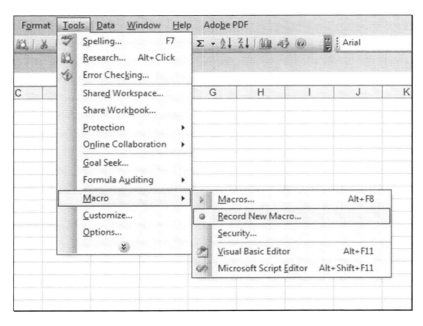

The following window will open:

In this window you will be asked to name the macro (it is recommended to change the default name provided by the program into a name that is significant and describes the code operation).

Rules for the Macro Names:

- The macro name must begin with a letter (not a number or other sign).
- Spaces are not allowed in a macro name (in other words, the macro should have a one-word name).
- You may use the underscore as a separator between two words, i.e. - Sum_Range.
- Do not choose Microsoft Excel's reserved names like 'print' or 'save'. To avoid problems that might arise due to reserved names, you can add the prefix 'My', i.e. My_Print to each macro.

- It is common to write the macro name in lowercase letters (although, if the macro name contain more than one word, you can combine uppercase for clarity, i.e. – SumRange).
- It is recommended to assign a name that accurately describes the meaning of the macro.

Note:

An error message will appear if you give a macro an illegal name.

In the next step you will have to choose where to store (save) the macro:

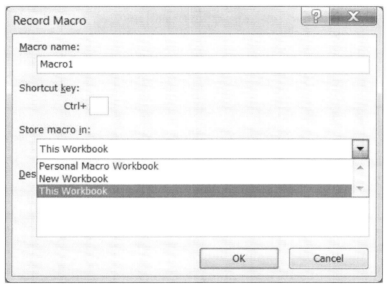

Personal Macro Workbook – the macro will be recorded automatically into the 'Personal.xlsb' file, which is loaded when Excel starts and is available for all workbooks (in the 2003 version, the file name is 'personal.xls').

This Workbook – the macro will be recorded in the current workbook.

New Workbook – the macro will be recorded in the new workbook.

You can choose a keyboard shortcut to run the macro.

Please note, there are many keyboard shortcuts in Microsoft Excel software, for example, Ctrl+S is used for saving, Ctrl+P is used for printing, etc.

While assigning a keyboard shortcut, the combination you choose will replace the keyboard shortcut action in the workbook where the code was saved. Therefore, it's preferable to use shortcuts that are used infrequently.

You can also add the 'Shift' key to the shortcuts by holding it down and simultaneously pressing the desired key (there is no need to press the 'Ctrl' key, which appears by default).

To confirm, click .

In the ribbon versions, the button  will be replaced by the button .

In the Excel 2003 version the 'recording macro' toolbar will appear:

This toolbar contains two buttons:
- **'Stop Recording'** – is used to stop the macro recording (if you don't stop recording when you've finished, any action

performed will also be recorded, including the action of running the macro itself…).

- '**Relative Reference**' – determines whether the macro you record will run as an 'absolute reference' (which means, it will run on the range of cells that were selected while the macro was recorded, regardless of your current position in the worksheet); or as a 'relative reference' (which means, relative to your position in the worksheet).

Note:

When the macro recording in the Excel 2003 version is completed, the recording toolbar will close automatically.

If you close the toolbar manually using the X sign at the top, it will not appear automatically the next time you want to record a macro.

In order to be display it again, start recording a new macro. Now - in a recording state - right-click on the toolbars and select **Stop Recording** (this toolbar appears in the toolbars list only when a macro is being recorded).

After the toolbar appears, you can stop recording (no need to save the macro).

Note: in the 'ribbon versions', those two buttons appear on the **Developer** tab in the **Code** group:

Relative Recording Exercise:

1. Open a new workbook

2. Select cell A1

3. Select a new macro recording

4. Give it the name 'YellowHello'

5. Store it in 'This workbook'

6. Assign to it the keyboard shortcut Ctrl+q

7. Click ⬚ OK ⬚.

8. Click the Relative Reference button ⬚ (this way the macro will run on any cell selected. Otherwise, the macro will always work on the range of cells selected when recording, regardless of the cursor position when running the macro)

9. Paint the cell background in yellow ⬚

10. Write "Hello"

11. Press **Enter** on the keyboard

12. Click the **Stop Recording** button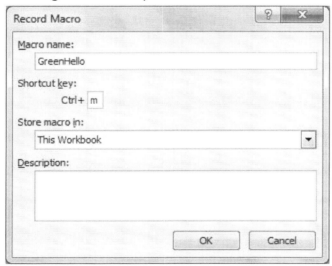

13. Now select any cell in the worksheet and run the macro using the key combination Ctrl+q

14. Save the workbook with the name 'Macro Recording' (if you record in the 'ribbon versions', save it with the .xlsm extension)

Absolute Recording Exercise

1. Open the file 'Macro Recording'

2. Select a new macro recording

3. Give the macro the name 'GreenHello'

4. Store it in 'This Workbook'

5. Assign to it the keyboard shortcut Ctrl+m

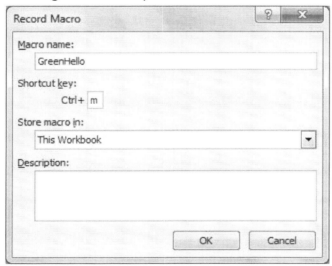

6. Click [OK]

7. If the Relative Reference button is active, deactivate it by clicking it again.

8. Select cell A1

9. Press Enter on the keyboard

10. Paint the cell background in green

11. Write "Hello"

12. Press Enter on the keyboard

13. Click the Stop Recording button

14. Delete the content and format of cell A2 (in the 'ribbon version' you can find this option under the Home tab -> Edit category, and in 2003 version select from the menu Edit -> Clear -> All.)

15. Select any cell in the worksheet and run the macro with the combination key Ctrl+m

Run a Macro

There are several ways to run the macro you have just recorded.

Note:

In the event that you are unable to run the macro due to a security level issue, follow the instructions in page 7.

Run a Macro in the 'Ribbon versions'

Run a macro from the Developer tab

1. On the **Developer** tab, in the **Code** group, click **Macros**
    to open a window with a recorded macros list.
2. Select the macro (you will recognise the name you assigned to it when it was recorded)
3. Click **Run**

Run a macro by pressing the assigned key combination

1. Select any cell in the worksheet
2. Press on the pre-determined key combination

Run a Macro by Assigning a Button from the Form Controls

1. On the **Developer** tab, click

2. Select a button

3. Draw a virtual square in the worksheet
4. The **Assign Macros** dialog box will appear
5. Select the desired macro
6. Click [OK]
7. Click the button to run the macro

Editing the Button

To edit the button, make sure it is framed (if you click on it while it is unframed, the macro associated with it will start running. To select it, if not framed, right-click on it).

A right-click will display the associated menu where you can edit the text, assign a different macro, etc.

Run a macro by adding a button to the Quick Access toolbar

1. Click the drop-down arrow in the quick access toolbar and select **More Commands**

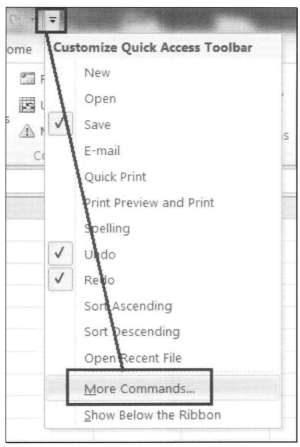

2. In the **Choose commands from** list, select **Macros**

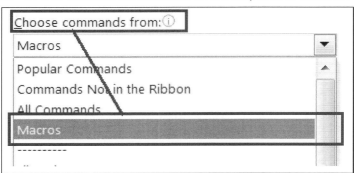

3. Select the desired macro

4. Click **Add**

5. Click OK

6. The button will appear on the quick access toolbar

Customize the Ribbon (only for 2010/2013 version)

Excel 2010/2013 allows the creation of new tabs and the addition of macro commands into custom groups in existing tabs.

Create a new tab:

1. Click the File tab

2. Under **Help**, Click Options

3. From the categories list select Customize Ribbon

4. Click New Tab

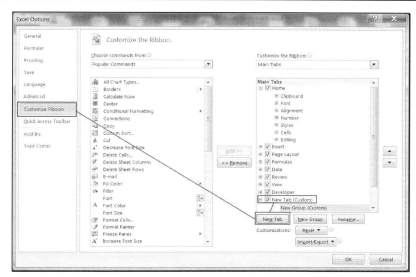

5. The new tab will be added to the ribbon tabs

6. You can rename the tab by clicking Rename...

Add a New Group (in a new tab or in an existing tab):

1. Click the **File** tab

2. Click **Options**

3. From the categories list select **Customize Ribbon**

4. Select the tab that you want to add a group to

5. Click **New Group**

6. A new group will be created in the tab you have selected:

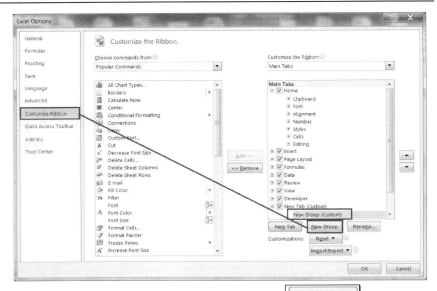

7. You can rename the group by clicking **Rename...**

Add a macro to the group

1. Click the **File** tab

2. Under **Help**, Click **Options**

3. From the categories list select **Customize Ribbon**

4. Click **Macros**

5. Select the desired macro from the list

6. Select the group that you want to add the macro to and click **Add >>**:

7. The button will be added to the group you have selected.

Run a Macro in Microsoft Excel 2003 version

Run a macro from the menu

1. Select **Tools -> Macro -> Macros**
2. Select the desired macro
3. Click **Run**

Run a macro by the key combination assigned while recording

1. Select any cell in the worksheet
2. Click on the key combination you have chosen

Run a macro by assigned button from the 'Forms' toolbar

1. Display the **Forms** toolbar (right-click on any toolbar and select **Forms** from the toolbars list)
2. Select **Button**
3. Draw a virtual square in the worksheet
4. **Assign Macro** dialog box will appear:

5. Select the desired macro and click OK
6. Deselect the button by clicking on any cell in the worksheet

7. Click on the button to run the macro

<u>Edit the Button</u>

To edit the button, make sure it is framed (if you click on it while it is not framed, the macro associated with it will start running. Right-click on it to select it).

A right-click will display the associated menu, where you can edit the text, assign a different macro, etc.

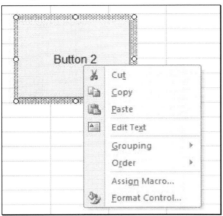

Run a macro by adding a button to the toolbar

1. Select **View -> Toolbars -> Customize**
2. On the **Commands** tab, select **Macros**
3. From the **Commands** box, drag the symbol into the desired toolbar
4. Right-click on the new symbol added to the toolbar, and select the menu **Assign Macro** (Note, in order to assign a macro, you must leave the **Customize** window open!)
5. Select the relevant macro from the open list
6. Click OK
7. Close the **Customize** window

Using Macro Recording for Process Efficiency

Many times during our work we deal with repetitive tasks. Instead of performing them again and again, we can record a macro to perform them automatically, with a single click!

For example, suppose we own a store and need to update the inventory periodically, we build a table in a fixed structure:

	A	B	C	D
1	Inventory			
2	Product	Price	Qty	Total
3	Computer	550	55	30250
4	Monitor	715	85	60775
5	Keyboard	35	40	1400
6	Mouse	15	60	900
7				

And design it as follow:

	A	B	C	D
1	Inventory			
2	Product	Price	Qty	Total
3	Computer	550	55	30250
4	Monitor	715	85	60775
5	Keyboard	35	40	1400
6	Mouse	15	60	900
7				

To make it more efficient, we record a macro that will perform the following actions:

1. Center the title

2. Change the title font size to 14

3. Add borders to the table

4. Color the titles

From now on, instead of performing four separate actions each time we want to design the data table, we can do it with a single click!

The macro recording:

1. Open the workbook "**Inventory.xls**" in the worksheet 'January'
2. Open the 'macro recording' window (see instructions see instructions on page 27)
3. Name the macro **'Inventory'** and store it in this workbook. (you can assign a keyboard shortcut to run it)
4. Make sure that the **Relative Reference** button is deactivated
5. Select the range A1:D1 and click the **Merge and Center** button
6. Change the font size to 14
7. Select the range A1:D6 and add a border to it
8. Select the range A2:D2 and add a background to it
9. Select the range A3:A6 and add a background to it
10. Click the '**Stop Recording**' button
11. Select worksheet 'February' and run the macro

Watching The Recorded Macro from the VB Editor and Improving it

Watching the Code

Watching a recorded code is a fundamental and easy way to learn how to write macro commands.

As you already learned in the chapter "Run a Macro" on page 35, there are several ways to run a macro.

An additional method is to run the macro directly from the VB editor (first, of course, make sure that there are macro commands in the editor)

Run a macro

1. Open the workbook "**Inventory.xls**"
2. Select worksheet 'March'

3. Click on the **Macros** button (in the 'ribbon versions'), or select from the menu **Tools → Macro → Macros** (in Excel 2003 version)
4. Make sure that the macro **Inventory** is selected
5. Click **Edit**
6. Now you can see all the previously recorded commands translated to VBA code
7. To run the macro click the **Run** button in the toolbar
   Or – select **Run → Run Sub**
   Or – press **F5** key on the keyboard

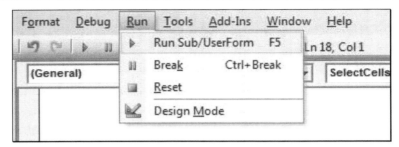

Running a macro step-by-step

Sometimes you would like to run the macro step-by-step (which means – one line after another) to test it

1. Open the workbook "**Cell Selection.xls**"
2. Go to worksheet 'Selection'

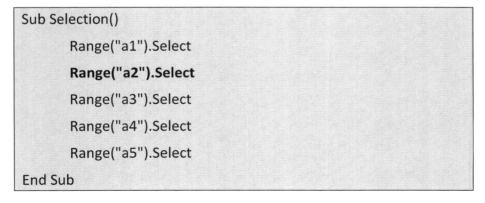

3. Click on the **Macros** button (in the 'ribbon versions'), or select from the menu **Tools → Macro → Macros** (in Excel 2003 version)
4. Make sure the macro **SelectCells** is selected
5. Click **Edit**
6. Press on **F8** key on the keyboard

```
Sub Selection()
        Range("a1").Select
        Range("a2").Select
        Range("a3").Select
        Range("a4").Select
        Range("a5").Select
End Sub
```

Please note, the highlighted line (in the VB editor it will be marked in yellow), is the next line to be executed.

In the example above, the A1 cell is already selected, and the **next** time you press on the F8 key cell A2 will be selected.

Stop running a macro

You can stop the action of the macro while it is running in a state of 'step-by-step' with the **Stop** button in the toolbar.

Sometimes it may be necessary to stop a macro from running despite the fact that it started running by order of the F5 key, for example – a macro that continues to run because it entered an infinite loop. The way to stop it is by pressing the **Esc** key or the keyboard shortcut **Ctrl+Break**.

Set a breakpoint

You can run a macro automatically up to a specific point, and then run it manually, to check the code snippet after the breakpoint (for example - a macro that runs a loop on 1000 rows in a worksheet, and then makes some calculations. Adding a breakpoint after the loop will save you from having to run the loop code manually 1000 times, but will allow you to check the calculations that follow it).

The VB editor enables the insertion of a breakpoint by clicking on the left gray border of the editor (or by pressing F9 while the cursor is placed at some point on the relevant code line).

You can add a breakpoint in a code line that contains any action, or in the macro name (you cannot add breakpoints in code lines that contain comments or declarations about variables)

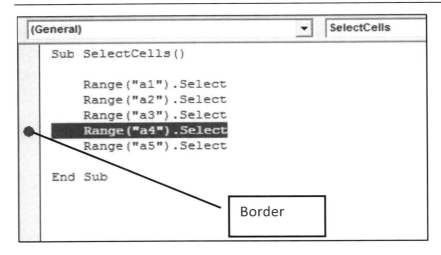

The line will be highlighted in red, and a red dot will appear next to it.

Now you can press the F5 key to run the code that will stop when it reaches the breakpoint; from there you can run it manually, step-by-step, by pressing F8, or run it to the end using the F5 key.

In the example above, pressing on F5 will run the code automatically for the first 3 lines (it will select cell A1, then cell A2, then cell A3, where it will stop).

Now you can continue running it manually by pressing F8, which will select cell A4, or by pressing F5, which will make it run to the end.

To remove the breakpoint, press on it again.

Exercise – breakpoint:
1. Open the workbook "**Cell Selection.xls**"
2. Select worksheet 'Selection'

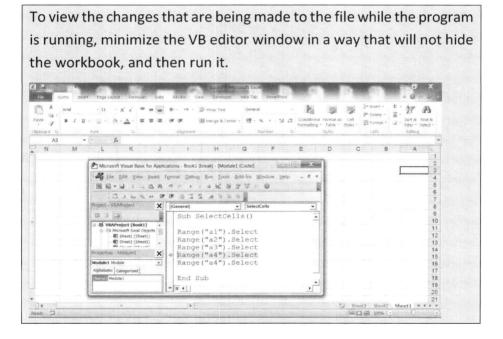

3. Click on the **Macros** button (in the 'ribbon versions'), or select from the menu **Tools → Macro → Macros** (in Excel 2003 version)

4. Make sure the macro **SelectCells** is selected

5. Click **Edit**

6. Add a breakpoint next to the 4th code line (which selects cell A4)

7. Press F5 on the keyboard

8. Check in the "Selection" worksheet which cell the cursor is located on

9. Continue running the code step-by-step by pressing F8

Tip:

To view the changes that are being made to the file while the program is running, minimize the VB editor window in a way that will not hide the workbook, and then run it.

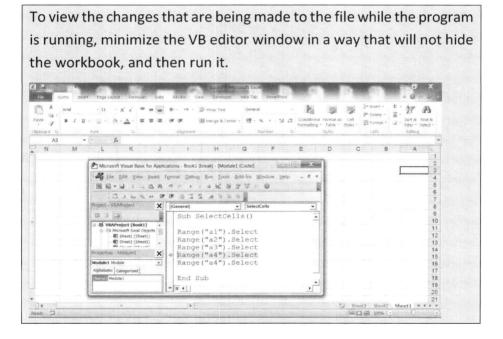

Code Improvement

When a macro is recorded, all of the properties of the object are also recorded, even those which were not changed.

For example, let's record a macro which changes the font size to 14. The macro recording will produce the following code:

```
Sub FontSize()
 With Selection.Font
        .Name = "Arial"
        .Size = 14
        .Strikethrough = False
        .Superscript = False
        .Subscript = False
        .OutlineFont = False
        .Shadow = False
        .Underline = xlUnderlineStyleNone
        .ThemeColor = xlThemeColorLight1
        .TintAndShade = 0
        .ThemeFont = xlThemeFontMinor
 End With
```

(Note, the code in the Excel 2003 version is somewhat different).

While checking the code we see many code lines with properties not chosen by us (i.e. the font name, or an underline).

Multiple lines slow the action of the macro, and make the code less distinct - this could be difficult to revise at a later stage.

Examining the code shows that all the features appearing in the tab **Font**, under the **format Cells** option, were recorded:

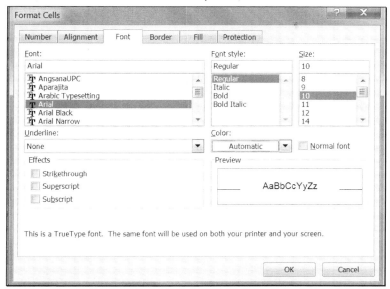

We can change the recorded code and delete all of those unnecessary properties by selecting the lines and pressing **the Delete** key.

Even if we are not yet familiar with the VBA code language, we can understand from the code itself which lines to delete and which to keep.

In the above example, the only property we changed is the font size, so all the other attributes (such as: font name, strikethrough, superscript, etc.) are unnecessary. The shorter code will look like this:

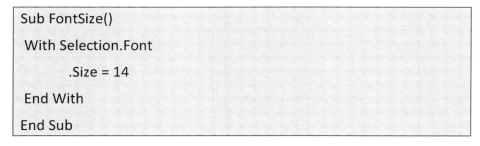

```
Sub FontSize()
  With Selection.Font
        .Size = 14
  End With
End Sub
```

Exercise - Improving the recorded code:

1. Open a new workbook
2. Write in cell A1 the word "Hello"
3. Click [🖫 Record Macro] (in the 'ribbon versions'), or select from the menu **Tools → Macro → Record New Macro...** (in Excel 2003 version)
4. Name it **Improve** and Press OK
5. Change the font type
6. Click [🔲 Stop Recording]
7. Click on the **Macros** button [Macros] (in the 'ribbon versions'), or select from the menu **Tools → Macro → Macros** (in Excel 2003 version)
8. Make sure that the macro **Improve** is selected
9. Click **Edit**
10. Watch the code
11. Delete all unnecessary code lines
12. Run the revised code and check whether it performs as required.

Writing Macro Commands in VB editor

After learning about the structure of the VB editor, how to record macros and even how to improve them, it's time to "get your hands dirty" and start writing your own codes.

Most of the macro commands will be written on two main levels:

1. **Module** level macro – this macro will be available to all worksheets of the workbook (file).
2. **Sheet** level macro – this macro will be available to the specific worksheet on which it was written (to make it work on other worksheets too, you must clearly specify it in the commands themselves).

Macro Commands' Structure

A VBA macro command is called a **Routine**

The routine starts with the word **Sub** followed by the macro name

Each routine ends with: **End Sub**.

Please note, as soon as you type the word Sub and the name of the macro, and press **Enter**, the command **End Sub** automatically appears, as well as the brackets after the macro name.

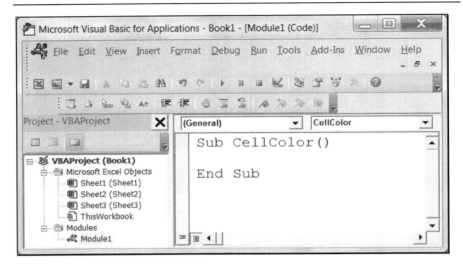

In the example above we notified the VB editor that we are about to write a macro named "CellColor".

Code Writing Conventions

In order to make the code clear, there are few writing conventions:

Comments – free text that describes the code.

To add a comment into the VBA code, type an apostrophe (') before the comment. The compiler will ignore what is written after the apostrophe, but the comments will help us to understand what we wrote, if we open the file at some future date (adding a comment can save hours of work trying to understand "what the poet meant" when he wrote the code ...).

The comment lines are automatically highlighted in green, to easily distinguish between them and the other lines of code.

A comment can be typed anywhere on the line (even next to the code line itself).

```
' This Macro colors the activecell

ActiveCell.Interior.Color = vbGreen
```

Tip:

Before deleting a code line it is recommended to mark it as a comment and check whether or not the code runs well without it.

In this manner, if we see that the code line is important (despite having thought it was unnecessary) we will not have to retype it, but merely delete the apostrophe (').

Use text indentation – pressing **TAB** on the keyboard causes text indentation of the line and allows us to see the code structure more clearly. The text indentation does not affect the code itself.

It is customary to use text indentation for **IF** command (page 91), **With** command (page 77) and while using loops (page 97).

Split lines – it is customary to split long lines by adding a space key and then an underline, as shown in the following example:

The command that colors the interior of cell A1 in yellow

```
Range("a1").Interior.Color = vbYellow
```

can be split into two lines:

```
Range("a1").Interior.Color = _
 vbYellow
```

The VB editor refers to the two lines as one continuous line.

Note the space before the underline!

Syntax

In order to write VBA codes, we must become familiar with the structure of the commands.

The command structure is, firstly, "**on what**" – in other words, what is the object we are referring to; only then comes the "**what**", meaning: what is the action (property or method) that we want to perform.

For example:

```
Range("a1").Copy
```

According to the explanation above:

"**On what**?" – on cell A1

"**What?** " – copy

Meaning: in VBA language we write the sentence as follows: "On cell A1 perform an action of copy".

The two parts of the command are separated by a dot (.).

Another example:

```
Range("a1").Interior.Color = vbRed
```

"**On what**? " - on the interior of cell A1

"**What**?" – color the cell in red

Tip:

```
The VB editor will allow auto-completion:
```

Start typing the object name and press on the keyboard shortcut Ctrl+Spacebar. If this is the only object starting with those letters, it will be completed automatically. If there are other objects, a list will appear, from which you can select the desired object by double-clicking it or by pressing the tab key, as illustrated in the following figure:

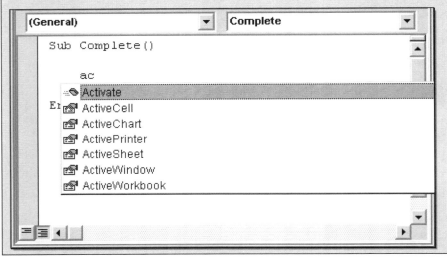

In the same way, you will know which methods and properties exist for each object: Press the keyboard shortcut Ctrl+Spacebar after the dot which separates the object from its methods and properties, as illustrated in the following figure:

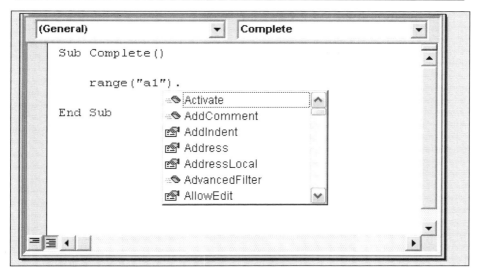

Recommendation:

Write the code in lowercase letters only.

If the code is correct, the compiler will automatically change the first letters of each command into uppercase letters when you move to the next line.

This way you can check if the syntax is written correctly.

If the commands, or some of them, remain in lowercase letters - there is an error in the syntax or the spelling.

Declaration on Variables and Objects

Will be done by the **Dim** command in the structure:

Dim x As Y

Dim MyName As String
Dim MyChart As Chart

For more details about the declaration, see page 73.

Applying a value to a variable

Is done by the symbol "="

```
Dim MyName As String

MyName = "Maayan Poleg"
```

You can apply values that appear in Microsoft Office settings to a variable:

```
Dim MyName As String

MyName = Application.UserName
```

In the above example we entered the username that was entered when installing the Microsoft Office package into the variable **MyName**, using the command **Application.UserName**

Applying an object to a variable

This can be done using the command **SET** and the symbol for 'equals' **"="**

In the following example, we insert the object **Application.WorksheetFunction**, which will allow the use of Microsoft Excel functions inside the code into the variable **WF**.

```
Set WF = Application.WorksheetFunction
```

Note: the variable **WF** is a variable that we created by ourselves.

It is recommended to give variables a meaningful name. In this case, the variable name is composed of the initials of the object.

For example:
If we want to use **Microsoft Excel** functions in the code, we can write this:

```
Range("b1").Value = _

Application.WorksheetFunction.Count(Range("a1:a10"))

Range("b2").Value = _

Application.WorksheetFunction.Average(Range("a1:a10"))

Range("b3").Value = _

Application.WorksheetFunction.Sum(Range("a1:a10"))
```

However, if we make a one-time insertion of the object
Application.WorksheetFunction into the variable **WF**, we can write
a shorter and more legible code:

```
Set WF = Application.WorksheetFunction

Range("b1").Value = WF.Count(Range("a1:a10"))

Range("b2").Value = WF.Average(Range("a1:a10"))

Range("b3").Value = WF.Sum(Range("a1:a10"))
```

Note:

The functions Count, Average and Sum are written in bold in order
to be easily identified by the readers of this guide. In practice, they
appear as regular text, not bold.

Ranges

One of the basic actions in Microsoft Excel applies to ranges on which we wish to conduct various processing.

Range can be a single cell, a sequence of cells, a column, a row, and even an entire worksheet.

The main commands that related to ranges are:

- Range
- ActiveCell
- Selection

Examples:

Code	Action
Range("b5").select	Selecting the cell B5 (Please note the quotation marks surrounding the cell name)
Range("b5:c10").Select	Selecting the range B5:C10
Range("b5", "c10").Select	Another way of applying to a range is by **selecting its ends**
Range(ActiveCell, "d3").Select	Selecting a range from the **Active Cell** to cell D3
Range("first").Select	Selecting a range by **using the name** "first" that was given earlier to a cell or to a range of cells in the worksheet
Range("first", "Second").Select	Selecting a range by using two names that were given earlier to two cells in the worksheet

Code	Action
Selection.Interior.Color = vbGreen	Coloring in green a range of cells that was selected earlier in the worksheet

Note:

Although it seems that the command **range("c2").select** is selecting cell C2, in fact it is selecting the cell in the second row and the third column, as the default reference point is A1.

Therefore, the next command:

Range("b5").Range("a2").Select

Selects the cell in the second row and the first column, according to the reference point **B5,** which means, cell **B6.**

Useful commands for selecting ranges in Microsoft Excel

The following list of commands select ranges **in the worksheet** by using different keyboard shortcuts.

The relevant VBA code is given alongside each command.

It is recommended to practice those commands in the worksheet itself, and also to record a macro and watch it.

- The keyboard shortcut **ctrl+down arrow** will move the cursor from the active cell to the last cell in the column, which is located before the nearest empty cell.

```
ActiveCell.End(xlDown).Select
```

- The keyboard shortcut **shift+ctrl+down arrow** will select the range from the active cell to the last cell in the column: (before the nearest empty cell).

```
Range(ActiveCell, ActiveCell.End(xlDown)).Select
```

- The keyboard shortcut **ctrl+up arrow** will move the cursor to the first row in the data range that contains the active cell which is located before the nearest empty cell (or to the top of the worksheet, if the first row of data is row number 1):

```
ActiveCell.End(xlUp).Select
```

- The keyboard shortcut **ctrl+shift+up arrow** will select the entire range, from the cursor location up to the empty cell above it (or to the top of the worksheet, if the first row of data is row number 1):

```
Range(ActiveCell, ActiveCell.End(xlUp)).Select
```

- The keyboard shortcut **ctrl+right arrow** or **left arrow** will take the cursor to the first or to the last data in a row (before the nearest empty cell), respectively:

```
ActiveCell.End(xlToRight).Select
ActiveCell.End(xlToLeft).Select
```

- The keyboard shortcut **ctrl+shift+ right arrow** or **left arrow** will select the data from the cursor location to the last cell in the column (before the nearest empty cell), from the right or from the left, respectively:

```
Range(ActiveCell, ActiveCell.End(xlToRight)).Select
```

- The keyboard shortcut **ctrl+asterisk (*)** will select the data table. It is customary to use the asterisk (*) key from the numeric section of the keyboard, but if you choose to use the asterisk above the number 8 from the upper row of numbers in the alpha-numeric section of the keyboard, press on the Shift key as well (**ctrl+shift+8**):

```
ActiveCell.CurrentRegion.Select
```

- The keyboard shortcut **Ctrl+A** will select the entire worksheet:

```
Cells.Select
```

- The keyboard shortcut **Ctrl+Home** will move the cursor to cell A1:

```
Range("A1").Select
```

- The keyboard shortcut **Ctrl+End** will move the cursor to the last data cell in the worksheet:

```
ActiveCell.SpecialCells(xlLastCell).Select
```

Tip:

To perform actions on the entire active data range in the worksheet, you can use the command UsedRange, for example:
ActiveSheet.UsedRange.Font.Size = 12

ActiveCell command

Enables performing actions on the active cell, without mentioning its specific location.

For example:

The command:

```
ActiveCell.Value = 5
```

Enters the value 5 into the active cell (the cell which the cursor is in).

Rows command

Enables you to refer to entire rows.

For example:

The command

```
Rows("2:3").Select
```

selects rows 2 and 3.

Columns command

Enables to refer to columns.

For example:

The command

```
Columns("C:D").Select
```

selects columns C and D.

Cells command

The '**cells**' command enables you select a cell given the row number and the column number. The importance of this command is that it enables referral to a cell in accordance with variables, and not with fixed data only.

Cells(row, column).Select

For example:

The command

```
Cells(5, 7).Select
```

selects cell G5.

Note:

Although in Mirosoft Excel the column number is specified first, followed by the row number, in the VB editor the row number should be specified first and then the column number.

Tip:

To select the last row in a contiguous data set (in column A, for example), use the following code:

```
Cells(Rows.Count, 1).End(xlUp).Select
```

Explanation:

The command Rows.Count returns the number of rows in the worksheet (in Excel 2003 version the number of rows is 65,536; and in the ribbon versions it is 1,048,576).

Therefore, we asked the program to go to the last cell of column A, and go up to the first row of data from the bottom.

To use the row number, you must enter the code into a variable and ask for the row number instead of selecting it. For example:

LastRow = Cells(Rows.Count, 1).End(xlUp).Row

(LastRow is a variable. We will discuss variables in the next chapter)

Offset command

Enables you refer to a cell, relatively to the active cell.

The command structure:

Offset (rows, columns)
For example:

Range("c5").Offset(3, 2).Select

The above command selects the cell which is located three rows down and two columns to the right of cell C5: that is, cell E8.

ActiveCell.Offset(-3, 2).Interior.Color = vbRed

The above command colors the cell which is located three rows up and two columns to the right of the active cell.

Selecting worksheets

You can refer to a worksheet by its name

Sheets("sheet2").Select

or by its serial number in the workbook:

```
Sheets(2).Select
```

Tip:
To select the last worksheet in the workbook, use the following code:

```
Sheets(Sheets.Count).Select
```

Explanation:
The command **Sheets.Count** returns the number of worksheets in the workbook; therefore, in the above code, the worksheet which has the same index number as the total number of worksheets in the workbook is selected.

Operations on ranges

Copy

The copy action is done by using the **copy** command

```
Range("a3").Copy
```

Paste

The paste action is done by using the **ActiveSheet.Paste** command

```
Range("a3").Copy
Range("a4").Select
ActiveSheet.Paste
Application.CutCopyMode = False
```

The above code copies the content of cell A3 and pastes it into cell A4. The command **Application.CutCopyMode = False** cancels the copying state (the surrounding lineal) of cell A3.

Tip:

You can use the following shortcut to paste the value into the desired range (in this case, into cell A4):

```
Range("a3").Copy Range("a4")
```

Alternatively, you can use the code:

```
Range("a4").Value = Range("a3").Value
```

Note:

Although both of the codes above yield the same result, their mode of performing the action is completely different:

In the first code we copied the value from cell A3 and pasted it into cell A4.

In the second code, however, we entered to cell A4 the value of cell A3 by using the "=" operation.

Naming a range

You can give names to cells or ranges from within the workbook itself, but you can also do it by using the command **Name**

For example:

```
Range("a1:a5").Name = "FirstRange"
Range("FirstRange").Select
```

In this code we gave the name "FirstRange" to the range A1:B5, and then we selected it according to its name.

Making calculations on ranges

You can perform mathematical calculations on cells, for example:

```
Range("a3").Value = Range("a3").Value - 3

Range("a4").Value = Range("a3").Value + 10
```

In the example above, cell A3 received a new value after a calculation that subtracted the number 3 from its current value.

Cell A4 received a value equal to the value in cell A3 plus 10.

Note:

Although in Microsoft Excel you cannot enter into cell a value that is based on a calculation that includes the cell itself ("circular reference"), it is possible when writing a VBA code, because the result of the calculation will appear in the cell as a value and not as a formula.

Exercise:

1. Open the workbook "Select Ranges.xls"
2. Write a macro for selecting the following ranges:
    a. the entire table
    b. the data in column A
    c. the data in the third row
    d. Range A2:C3

Variables

A variable is a kind of "memory stack" whose purpose is to store data temporarily.

The "stack" contents can change while the code is running.

It is customary to declare the names and also the types of variables at the beginning of the code.

Rules for naming variables:

- A variable name must start with a **letter**.
- The name of a variable cannot contain spaces.
- You cannot use the same name as the name of the macro.
- You cannot use reserved names such as **save** and **print.**
  To avoid problems arising from the use of reserved names, you can add the suffix 'My' to the variable name, for example – MySum.
- It is recommended to use a name which accurately describes the meaning of the variable, for example – name the variable that stores the number of the last row in a specific column 'LastRow'.
- You can use the underline to combine two words, for example - Last_Row. It is customary to use lowercase and uppercase letters to make reading easier.

- An incorrectly typed variable will create a new variable. For example: let's say you gave a variable the name **MyRng** and later on you mistakenly wrote **MyRange** - a new variable with this name will be created automatically.

- Before the code starts running, the variables get a primary value:
  Variables that were declared as numeric will get the value 0,

and variables that were declared as text will get the value "empty".

- When you stop running the code, the value of the variable is automatically reset and is not saved in memory (in other words, when the code stops running – all the "memory stacks" are emptied of their content).

Note:

Naming a variable with an illegal name will color the line in red.

Types of Variables

There are many types of variables. We will discuss only the most important ones:

Numeric variable

Variable Type	Size (Bytes)	Values Range
Byte	1	0-255
Boolean	2	True or False
Integer	2	(-32,768)-(32,767)
Long	4	(-2,147,483,648)-(2,147,483,647)

Other variables

Double – Enables the storing of decimal numbers

String – Enables the storing of text strings

Range – Enables the storing of ranges

Date – Enables the storing of dates

Variant – "super variable" – stores all of above variables in it.

However, to save memory space, use the smallest variable that is still able to contain the values needed.

Note:

you do not have to declare variables, but if they are not declared, the variable type will be determined as VARIANT by default, which uses a lot of memory space.

> To obligate the users to declare variables in a certain module, you can add the command **Option Explicit** at the top of the module, which will prevent the code from running if there are undeclared variables.

Declaration of variables is done by the command **Dim**

For example:

```
Dim LastRow As Integer
Dim Rng As Range
```

In this code we defined the variable **LastRow** as an Integer

While the variable **Rng** we defined as a Range

Why you should obligate the user to declare variables?

Although it is not obligatory to declare variables, avoiding the declaration can cause problems due to the fact that each time the compiler encounters a variable it does not recognize, it creates a new one.

The next example will help to clarify this:

We have a product at a certain price, and we wish to raise the price by 10%. We have to multiply the old price by 1.1, therefore we wrote the following code:

```
OldPrice = 30
NewPrice = price * 1.1
```

We gave the variable **OldPrice** a primary value of 30.

Then, we wanted to get the new value of the product in the variable **NewPrice**, but didn't realize we had used the variable **Price** instead of **OldPrice**.

Due to the fact that the variable Price is unrecognized, it is automatically created and receives the value 0; therefore the multiplication result is 0 and not 33 as expected.

If we were obligating the user to declare variables, we would get an error message, when the compiler encountered the variable **Price**.

You can declare a variable without declaring its type:

Dim LastRow

In this case the editor will prevent us from using the variables incorrectly, but the variable type will be determined as a Variant, which uses a lot of memory space.

View the variables while running the code

While running the code in a 'step-by-step' mode you can view the values that each variable receives.

Locals window

Displays a list of all variables in the procedure.

To show the window, select **View → Locals Window**

Expression	Value	Type
⊞ Module1		Module1/Module1
I	5	Variant/Integer
J	5	Variant/Integer

You can see the variables change during the running of the code in a 'step-by-step' mode

Watch window

Enables viewing the selected variables while the code is running.

Add variables to the window:

1. Right-click on the desired variable (from within the code)
2. Select **Add Watch**

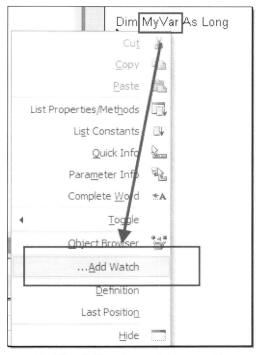

3. The following window will open:

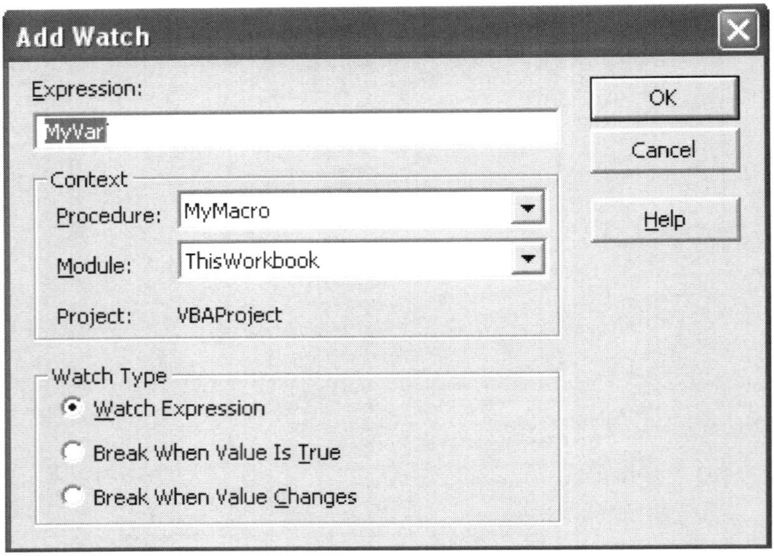

4. Make sure you selected the right variable
5. Click 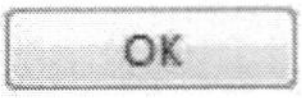

6. The variable will appear in the window, as shown in the illustration below:

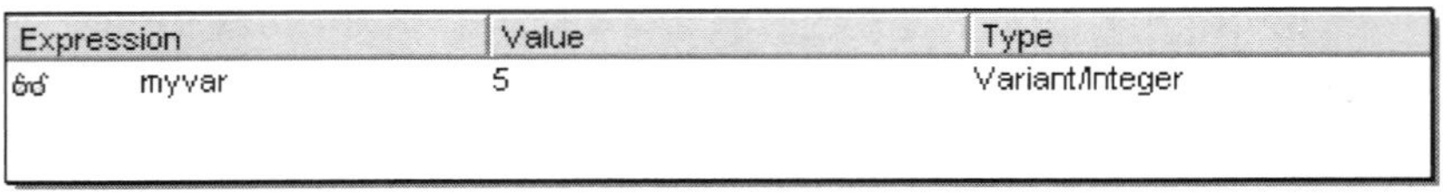

'With' Command

Sometimes we are required to perform several actions on the same range.

In this case, we can write a macro like the one in the following example, which performs four different actions on the cell A1:

```
Range("a1").Interior.Color = vbYellow

Range("a1").Font.Bold = True

Range("a1").Font.Color = vbRed

Range("a1").Value = Range("a1").Value * 2
```

However, the VB editor enables shorter and clearer writing by using the "**With** Command", which assigns all the commands to the selected object, specifying its name only once.

Syntax:
```
With Object
        .command
        .command
End With
```

note to the dot (.) at the beginning of each command line.

```
With Range("a1")
        .Interior.Color = vbYellow
.Font.Bold = True
.Font.Color = vbRed
.Value = Range("a1").Value * 2
End With
```

In the sample above we referred to cell A1 only once, and then performed different actions on it.

In terms of performance, there is no difference between the first code and the second one, but the second code saves typing and looks clearer.

Strings

String is a textual sequence on which you can make different manipulations.

Syntax rules:

- Each string will be surrounded by quotation marks. For example – "Hello".
- Strings concatenation or concatenating a string to a variable, will be done by the symbol "**&**", with spaces before and after. For example: "hello" & "goodbye".

Important commands for strings:

Len – returns the string length.
Syntax:
Len (text)
Example:
Return the length of the string Hello World

```
MyLen = Len("Hello World")
```

Return the length of the string in cell C3:

```
MyLen = Len(Range("c3"))
```

Ucase – Converts the letters of the string to uppercase
Syntax:
Ucase (text)

Example:
Converts the letters of the string into uppercase, in the active cell.

```
ActiveCell.Value = UCase(ActiveCell.Value)
```

LCase - converts the letters of the string into lowercase

Syntax:

Lcase (text)

Left – returns a fixed number of characters from the left side of the string.

Syntax:

Left (text, length)

Example:

Return to cell A2 five characters from the left side of the string in cell A1:

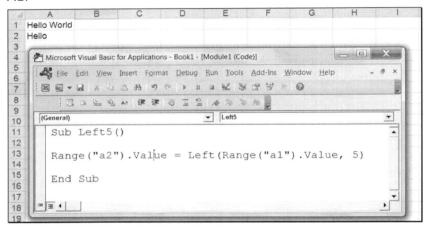

Right – returns a fixed number of characters from the right side of the string.

Syntax:

Right (text, length)

Mid – returns a fixed number of characters from the middle of the string.

Syntax:

Mid (text, start [, length])

Note that the 'length' argument specifies the desired length of returned string, and it is optional. If it is omitted, the string that will be returned is the one that starts from the place specified in the second argument, and ends at the last character of the string.

Instr – returns the position of one string inside another string.
Syntax:
Instr (start, where, what)
For example:

Find the 'space' character location inside the string "Hello World":

```
MySpace = InStr(1, "Hello World", " ")
```

The variable MySpace will get the value 6, because the 'space' character is the sixth character of the string "Hello World".

Instead of writing the string in a code line, you can refer the search to a cell in the worksheet:

```
MySpace = InStr(1, Range("a1"), " ")
```

InStrRev – returns the location of one string inside another, when the search begins from the end of the string.
Syntax:
InStrRev (where, what, start)

For example:
Search for the letter "o" in the string "Hello World", beginning from the end:

```
MyO = InStrRev("Hello World", "o")
```

Note:

the search is done from the end of the string, but the result is the location from the beginning of the string, and in this case, the variable MyO will receive the value 8.

You can also refer the search to a cell in the worksheet, instead of writing the string inside the code.

Replace – replaces one string with another.

Syntax:

Replace (string, sub-string to replace, replace with)
For example:

Replace the word 'big' with the word 'small':

```
MyRplc = Replace("I'm Big", "Big", "Small")
```

You can also refer the search to a cell in the worksheet, instead of writing the string inside the code.

Date and Time

Dates are stored in the VB editor as decimal numbers, starting from the 1st of January 100 till the 31st of December 9999.

Note:

although the VB editor enables dates to be used from the year 100, Microsoft Excel software does not enable dates prior to the year 1900.

When you enter a date composed of numerals, surround it with the symbol #:

```
MyDt = #12/31/2013#
```

When you enter a date as a string, surround it with quotation marks:

```
MyDt = "December 31, 2013"
```

The command that returns today's date is **Date** (the same as the function 'Today()' in Microsoft Excel).

The following code will enter today's date into cell A1:

```
Range("a1").Value = Date
```

The following code will enter the date 7 days from today into cell A1:

```
Range("a1").Value = Date + 7
```

Time

This command returns the time.

The following code will enter the time into the variable MyTm:

```
MyTm = Time
```

TimeSerial

This command returns the time in an hours:minutes:seconds structure.

Syntax:

TimeSerial(hh, mm, ss)

The following code returns the time 1:25:00 into the variable MyTm:

```
MyTm = TimeSerial(1, 25, 0)
```

The following code returns the time that will apply, three hours, twenty minutes and fifteen seconds from now, into the variable MyTm:

```
MyTm = Now + TimeSerial(3, 20, 15)
```

Interaction With the User

One of the most powerful options of VB editor is the ability to create interaction with the user while running the code, by displaying messages to the user and receiving data from him.

MsgBox

A message box enables the display of messages to the user.

Command structure:

MsgBox ("Enter your text here")

Example:

```
MsgBox ("Hello")
```

Useful symbols for the MsgBox

The symbol "**&**" is concatenating text strings.

As in the following code, for example:

```
MsgBox ("Hello " & Application.UserName)
```

The following message will appear:

Note the space after the word "Hello".

The space was added inside the quotation marks after the word "Hello", in order to add a space between the two parts of the message.

> The command **Appliction.UserName** returns the username that was entered during the installation of the Microsoft Excel package.

The command **VbNewLine** allows the creation of a new row inside the message box.

For example:

> MsgBox ("Hello " & vbNewLine & Application.UserName)

The following message will appear:

A message box that allows decision-making

As we saw, the message box allows the user to receive messages. However, you can use the message box to enable the user to choose from several existing options, such as "OK" or "Cancel".

Because in this type of message box we receive information from the user, we have to store it in a variable for a future use.

Syntax:

MyMsg = MsgBox ("Your Text", vbButtons)

For example:

```
msginfo = MsgBox("Do you want to proceed?", vbYesNo)
If msginfo = vbNo Then
        Exit Sub
End If
```

In the example above we used a message box of vbYesNo type, which displays two option buttons:

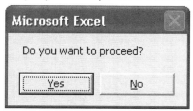

The returned value will be entered into the variable MsgInfo.

Now we can act according to the result received in the variable, usually by using the command **If** (which will be taught in the next chapter).

Button options:
- vbOKOnly
- vbOKCancel
- vbAbortRetryIgnore
- vbYesNoCancel
- vbYesNo
- vbRetryCancel

Warning options:

-    vbCritical

-    vbExclamation

-    vbInformation

Note:

Warning options are used for display purposes only!

You can combine buttons and warnings inside a message box:

MyMsg = MsgBox("Quit Without Saving?", vbOKCancel + vbExclamation)

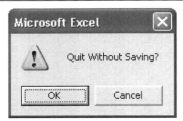

Pay attention to the "+" symbol that is used to connect the two options!

InputBox

Input box is used to receive information from the user.

The information will be stored in a variable, for future use.

The command structure:

MyVar = InputBox ("Your Text")

For example:

UsrNm = InputBox("What is your name?")

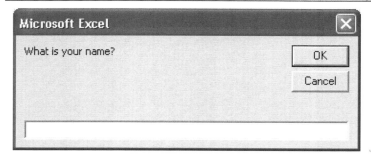

The following code requests the user to enter his/her name, and then returns a message box with the value that the user entered into the variable UsrNm:

```
UsrNm = InputBox ("What Is Your Name?")
MsgBox ("Hello " & UsrNm)
```

Explanation:

The value that was entered by the user using the InputBox will be entered into the variable UsrNm.

In the second stage, a message will be displayed to the user by the MsgBox command, showing the concatenation of the string "Hello" with the value that was store in the variable UsrNm.

Adding a title to the inputbox:

To change the title from the 'Microsoft Excel' default title, use the following structure:

```
UsrNm = InputBox("What Is Your Name?", "Names")
```

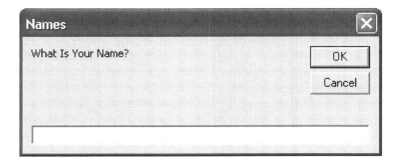

Conditions

Conditions enable decision-making based on data obtained while running the code.

The basic condition command structure

If <u>condition</u> then

      Commands for execution

End if

Meaning: the condition is examined whether it received a "True" or "False" value. The operating instructions will apply only if the value "True" was received.

Comparison operators

Operators	Meaning
=	Equal
<>	Not equal
>	Bigger than...
<	Smaller than...
>=	Bigger than or equal to...
<=	Smaller than or equal to...
And	Gets "True" value only when all parts of the equation are satisfied
Or	Gets "True" value when one part or both parts of the equation are satisfied
Not	Gets "True" value only when the relevant part of the equation is not satisfied

Examples:

The following code checks whether the value in cell A1 is bigger than the value in cell A2.

In the event that it is bigger, a message box will appear indicating "a1 is bigger than a2".

```
If Range("a1").Value > Range("a2").Value Then
 MsgBox ("a1 is bigger than a2")
End If
```

The above code checks the truth of the statement A1>A2. If it is - meaning that the value in cell A1 is actually bigger than the value in cell A2 - the operating instructions will be carried out and, in this case, a text box with the sentence "a1 is bigger than a2" will appear.

In case it is a false sentence, meaning that the value in cell A1 is not bigger than the value in cell A2, the message box will not appear.

Note: testing conditions is not limited to numeric values only.
The following code checks whether the username that was entered is Maayan; In the event that it is, a message will appear.

```
UsrName = InputBox("What is your name?")
If UsrName = "Maayan" Then
 MsgBox ("Hello Maayan ")
End If
```

Note, texts comparison is case sensitive. Therefore, if the name "MAAYAN" was entered, the condition will get the value "false"; after all, we compared it to the string "Maayan", therefore, contrary to our expectations, the desired text box will not appear.

We can solve it in two ways:

- **Comprehensively,** by adding the command **Option Compare Text** at the top of the module; that will cancel the case sensitivity of all module codes.

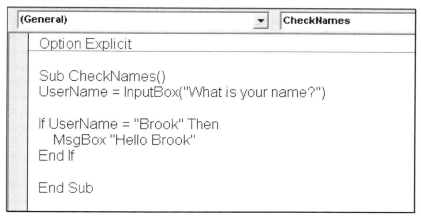

- **For a specific command** – by using LCase or UCase for the templates' structure comparison.

The decision of which approach to take depends on the purpose of the strings comparison – if, in most parts of the code, the letter type is important, then it is better to avoid using the command **Option Compare Text** which would cancel the case sensitivity of all module commands.

Complex condition

Sometimes we will have to execute one kind of instruction when the condition is "True" and a different instruction when it is "False".

For that we must use the structure: If... Then...Else

Syntax:

If condition Then

       Commands for execution

Else

       Commands for execution

End if

Example:

In the following code we ask the user to enter his/her name. If the name entered is Maayan, the user will get the message "Hi Maayan". If a different name is entered, the message will be "I wish you were Maayan"

```
UsrName = InputBox("What is your name?")
If UsrName = "Maayan" Then
        MsgBox ("Hi Maayan")
Else
        MsgBox ("I wish you were Maayan")
End If
```

When more than two conditions exist, you can use Elself

Example:

```
UsrName = InputBox("What is your name?")
If UsrName = "Maayan" Then
        MsgBox "Hi Maayan"
ElseIf UsrName = "Dan" Then
        MsgBox "Hi Dan"
Else
        MsgBox "I wish you were Maayan"
End If
```

Example for using VbButtons:

```
Proc = MsgBox("Do you want to proceed?", vbYesNo)
If proc = vbYes Then
        ActiveCell.Value = 5
End If
```

Explanation:

The value that was chosen by the VbYesNo button was entered into the variable Proc.

If the user clicked '**Yes**', the value 5 will be entered into the active cell (and if '**No**' was clicked, nothing will happen).

Loops

One of the most useful tools of code-writing is the loop structure, which enables the code to be run a number of times in succession, according to the data entered.

For example, if we have a large database, and we want to run a test on a large number of data records, we can write a code line for each data record. However, it is easier and more correct to write the code line only once and run it in a loop over all of the data records.

There are two main loop types:

- The **Do** loop type, which allows the code to be repeated under certain conditions.
- The **For** loop type, which allows the code to be repeated a predetermined number of times.

Do-Loop

This loop enables the same code lines to be repeated under certain conditions, when the number of repetitions is unknown.

There are two types of Do-Loop loops.

Do-While loop

This loop enables the same code lines to be repeated **as long as** a certain condition exists.

```
Range("a1").Select
Do While ActiveCell.Value <> ""
        ActiveCell.Value = ActiveCell.Value * 2
        ActiveCell.Offset(1, 0).Select
Loop
```

Explanation:

In the above example, the code multiplies the value of the active cell by 2, then selects the cell below it and multiplies it, and so on, as long as the active cell is not empty.

If an empty cell will be selected while the code is running, the code will stop running (even if other cells with values are located below the empty cell).

Do-Until loop

This loop enables the same code lines to be repeated **until** a certain condition occurs.

```
Range("a1").Select
Do Until ActiveCell.Value = ""
        ActiveCell.Value = ActiveCell.Value * 2
        ActiveCell.Offset(1, 0).Select
Loop
```

Explanation:

In the above example, the code multiplies the active cell value by 2, then selects the cell below it and multiplies it, and so on, until it arrives at an empty cell.

When an empty cell will be selected, the code will stop running (even if other cells with values are located below the empty cell).

In effect, both codes are performing the same action, but with a different approach – in the first code the condition is: **as long as the cell is not empty**, and in the second code the condition is: **until it arrives at an empty cell**.

For-Next loop

This loop allows a code to be repeated a pre-determined number of times.

The loop structure:

For counter = X To Y

       Commands for execution

Next counter

Example:

```
For i = 1 To 10
        MsgBox (i)
Next i
```

The above loop uses the variable i to receive values from 1-10. Each time the variable gets value, a message box with the value of the variable appears.

By default, the loop counter increases by 1 each time, but you can set the number of "steps" by using the command **Step**:

```
For i = 2 To 10 Step 2
        MsgBox (i)
Next i
```

another example:

```
For i = 10 To 2 Step -2
        MsgBox (i)
Next i
```

Example for creating the multiplication table by using a 'For' loop:

```
For i = 1 To 10
        For j = 1 To 10
                Cells(i, j) = i * j
        Next j
Next i
```

Explanation:

In this code there are two variables: i and j, which receive values from 1-10.

Moreover, there are two **For** loops: internal and external.

Every time the external loop (i) counter increases by 1, the internal loop (j) runs 10 times and enters the multiplication of the variables i and j into the cell, the position of which is determined by the variables i and j values.

Recommendation:

Run the following code step-by-step and use the Watch window to see the changes of the values.

Note that there is no need to select the cell by using the command **select** in order to insert a value into it!

(In fact, one of the differences between an experienced programmer and a novice is the number of times the command **select**...is used) .

Tip:

You can use variables to determine beginning and end values:

ShtCnt = ActiveWorkbook.Sheets.Count

For i = 1 To ShtCnt

       Sheets(i).Range("a1").Value = Sheets(i).Name

Next i

In the above example we used the variable ShtCnt to determine the numbers of the worksheets in the workbook. Then we used the For-Next loop, which ran as many times as the number of worksheets and fed its name into cell A1, at each of the worksheets.

For-Each loop

For-Each loop enables performing actions on collections, which gather objects of the same type.

A collection of worksheets, for example, gathers all of the worksheets in it; a collection of charts, gathers all of the charts in it; a range gathers cells in it and so on.

Syntax:

For each <u>object</u> in <u>collection</u>
        Commands for execution
Next

Example for creating a multiplication table by using a For-Each loop:

```
For Each CL In Range("a1:j10")
        CL.Value = CL.Row * CL.Column
Next
```

Explanation:

In this command, the macro goes through each of the cells in the specified range and multiplies the row number of the cell by its column number.

The VB editor "knows" that the object that builds the collection "range" is a cell, therefore it "understands" that the variable CL is a "cell". Therefore, for the collection's objects, you can use any name (as long as it is not a reserved name, and preferably it should be a meaningful one), in order to represent them.

In the same way, we gave the object that builds the collection of worksheets the name SH (which stands for a single worksheet).

```
For Each SH In Sheets

        SH.Tab.ColorIndex = 40

Next
```

the macro above colors the tab of the workbook pink.

Example for feeding the worksheet name into cell A1

```
For Each SH In Sheets

        SH.Range("a1").Value = SH.Name

Next
```

As you see, in some cases you can choose between a For-Next loop or a For- Each loop to execute the same actions.

Using the For-Each loop is usually shorter and more elegant.

User Defined Functions

Through VBA programming you can develop functions to use with Microsoft Excel.

The function purpose is to return a value, and it must be written at the module level and not at the worksheet level.

If you wish to save functions so that they will be available to all workbooks and not just the current one, you should save them in the **Personal.xlsb** workbook (in Excel 2003 version save them in the 'personal.xls' file)

> Note that the 'Personal.xlsb' workbook does not exist until you record a macro and save it in that workbook. After this one-time action, the recorded macro can be deleted, and you can save all the functions that you want to be available for all workbooks.

Syntax:

Function <u>function name</u> (x, y)

      Commands for execution

End Function

Explanation:

Unlike codes, which begin with the word **Sub**, functions begin with the word **Function** and end with the phrase **End Function.**

Enter the number of possible arguments in the brackets.

The following example shows a developed function that divides two variables:

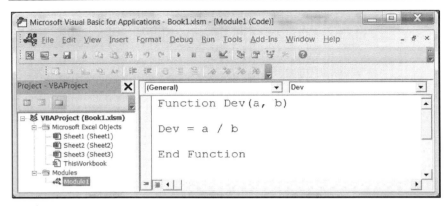

Explanation:

We announced to the VB editor that we are about to write a function named Dev, which has two arguments (a,b)

Then, we defined the action that we want to perform on those variables.

Note:

The name of the function must be identical to that of the variable where the result will be inserted (contrary to routines where variable names must be different from that of the routine itself).

How to run the function from a Microsoft Excel workbook?

There are two ways to run the function:

By the Insert function button:

1. In the 'Ribbon versions' select **Formulas → Insert function**

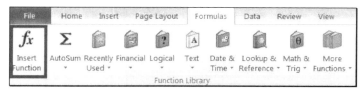

In Excel 2003 version select the menu **Insert →Function**

2. Select the category **User Defined**

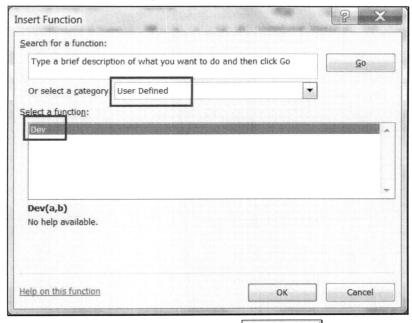

3. Select the function and Click OK

4. The following window will open:

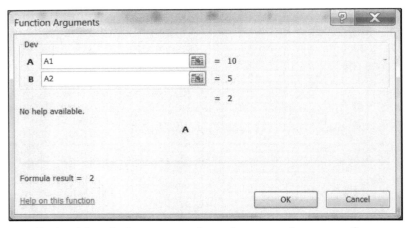

5. In this window enter the relevant values or references.

6. To finish, Click [OK]

By directly typing the function name in the worksheet:

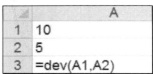

	A
1	10
2	5
3	=dev(A1,A2)

Note:

if you enter the value 0 into parameter b (the second parameter the function gets), you will get a **value** error (and not the Div/0 error that usually appears in the worksheet itself when it is divided by 0):

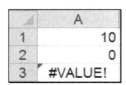

	A
1	10
2	0
3	#VALUE!

Tip:

You cannot check a function by running it directly from the VB editor.

To overcome this problem, you can add a breakpoint at the beginning of the function and then run it from the workbook.

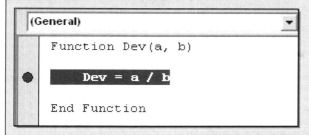

In this way, the function execution will stop, the VB editor will open and then you can continue running it using either F5 or F8.

When the test finishes, don't forget to remove the breakpoint.

Error handling

There are three main types of errors handled by the software.

- **Syntax Error** – appears when the code doesn't follow the VBA syntax rules. In this case, the line will be colored in red when we move to the next line.

  In the following example the second code line was colored in red, since the closing quotation marks were missing after the cell name.

  ```
  Sub MyErrors()
  range("a1).select
  End Sub
  ```

  We must detect the problem that caused the error by ourselves.

- **Compilation Error** – appears when the command structure is wrong, for example – a **For** loop without the suffix **Next**, or **If** command without the ending line **End IF**.

  In the following example we wrote a **For** loop, but we haven't closed it with the **Next** command. While trying to run the code, this error message will appear:

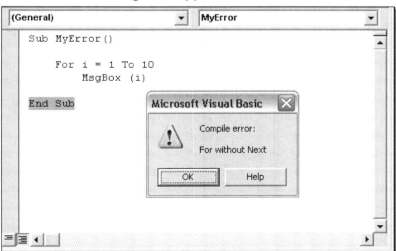

Note, the compiler checks the code **before** it starts running and notes an error.

- **Run-Time Error** – appears **while** the code is running as a reaction to a command that cannot be performed, such as referring to a worksheet that does not exist. When this kind of error is detected, the code stops running and an error message appears.

   In the following example we asked to select the cell above the active cell. When we selected cell A1, we received an error message, because there are no cells above it.

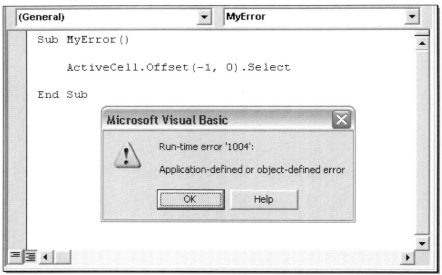

As we have seen, in that command there was neither a syntax error nor an error in structure; therefore we were unable to detect the problem before running the code.

Handling Run-time errors is done by the command **On Error**:

On Error GoTo Label

This command refers to another part in the code which is supposed to handle that kind of error.

```
On Error GoTo line1
ActiveCell.Offset(-1, 0).Select
Exit Sub


line1:
If ActiveCell.Row = 1 Then
MsgBox "First Line"
End If
```

In the above code we refer the editor to the label 'line1' where we will display a message box to the user which clarifies that he is in the first row.

Note:

because the code is running linearly, it will continue running to "line1" according to the order of the code lines, even if no error was detected; in the above example, a message box will appear. Therefore, we added the command **Exit Sub** after the appropriate cell selection, which causes the code to stop running.

Although you can "jump" from one part to another while running the code, it is recommended to use this option only for handling errors, since it makes it impossible to revise the code.

To be able to "jump", you must add the code label with a colon at the end, and call it by name with the command GoTo, as shown in the example above.

On error resume next

In some cases we would like to comprehensively ignore Run-time errors.

To do so we will write the command **On error resume next** before a line that might contain an error. This will instruct the compiler to ignore errors, even if they exist.

Be sure to use this option only when you are prepared to accept the errors that will arise while the code is running.

Sometimes we might want to use this command in one part of the code, but not in other parts.

To cancel the command, use the command **On Error GoTo 0**.

An Event Macro

The VBA is an event-oriented language.

An event macro enables a macro to run automatically following certain events made in the workbook, such as opening, closing, saving, double-clicking, changing and more.

A macro of this kind is written at the worksheet level or at the workbook level (**ThisWorkbook** in the explorer), and not at the module level.

An event macro that will be written at the worksheet level will apply only to the worksheet it was written in, while an event macro at the workbook level will apply to all the worksheets in the file.

Note:

The macro names are pre-determined and cannot be changed.

An event macro at the worksheet level

1. Double-click the name of the desired worksheet in the object explorer.

2. In the left upper window select **WorkSheet**:

3. Now you can choose the event that will run the code automatically from a list in the right window.

The following table lists the important events in the worksheet:

Change :This macro will run automatically when a value in one of the worksheet cells will change

SelectionChange :This macro will run automatically when cells in the worksheet will be selected

Note, when selecting an event macro of **Change** type, the reserved word **Target** will appear inside the brackets.

Target represents the range that triggered the event (contrary to ActiveCell that represents the active cell)

Run the following code to see the difference between **Target** and **ActiveCell**

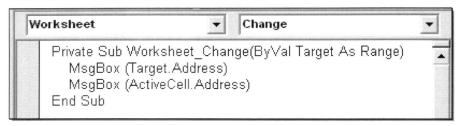

An event macro at the workbook level

1. Double-click **ThisWorkBook**.
2. In the left upper window select **Workbook**:

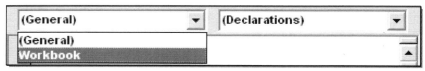

3. Now you can choose the event which will run the code automatically from the list in the right window.

The following table lists the important events in the workbook:

Open: This macro will run automatically when we open the workbook

BeforeClose: This macro will run before the file is closed (it enables the running of tests which prevent the file from being closed if pre-determined conditions were not fulfilled)

NewSheet: This macro will run when a new worksheet will be added

BeforeSave: This macro will run before the file is saved

Deactivate: This macro will run when the workbook will become non-active (for example, when selecting a different file)

SheetChange: This macro will run when a change will occur in one of the worksheets

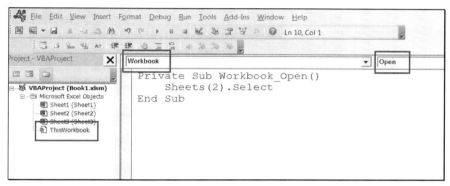

The above event macro is of **Workbook_open** type: in other words, this macro runs when the workbook is opened.

In this case, when the file opens, the second worksheet will open automatically.

Tip:

The following code cancels the workbook closure

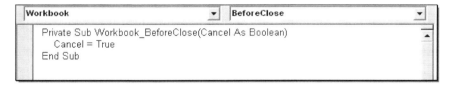

Supplements

How to protect the code from being viewed or copied?

The protection blocks the unpermitted user from entering the code, looking at it or changing it.

1. Right-click on the project window (you can click anywhere in the project area)
2. Select **VBAProject Properties**
3. In the opened window select the **Protection** tab

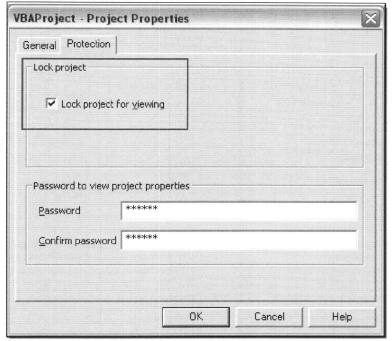

4. Check **Lock project for viewing**
5. Enter password
6. Any attempt to enter the VBA editor will open a window requesting a password

Note:

The protection will only take effect after closing and reopening the file.

Recommendation:

It is recommended to use a password that you can easily remember when you will try to view the code in the future...

Increase the macro running speed

Long codes that work on a big range of data slow the computer processing power.

One of the main reasons for that is that every action executed while the code is running actually takes place on the screen.

We can make the code run without the screen refreshing:

At the beginning of the code write the command:

```
Application.ScreenUpdating = False
```

Don't forget to return the screen refresh at the end of the code by the command:

```
Application.ScreenUpdating = True
```

Calling a macro from another macro

You can run a macro from another macro. The call is made by writing the other code name inside the current one.

For example:

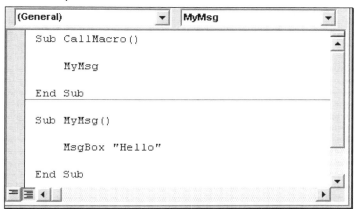

In the above example, running the code **CallMacro** will call the code MyMsg, which will display a text box with the word "Hello".

Using the Microsoft Excel functions in a macro

Sometimes we want to use Excel functions in the macro we write. It is done by the Application.WorksheetFunction code, followed by the desired function name

For example:

```
Range("a11").Value = _

Application.WorksheetFunction.Average(Range("a1:a10"))
```

Using colors

There are few methods for choosing a color:

- By using the color name, for example vbRed

- By using the index number of the color, for example ColorIndex=3

```
Range("a1").Interior.Color = vbRed

Range("a2").Interior.ColorIndex = 26

Range("a3").Font.Color = vbBlue

Range("a4").Font.ColorIndex = 10
```

Basic list of colors

Index	Color
1	Black
2	White
3	Red
4	Green
5	Blue
6	Yellow

To find all the color codes (56 colors) you can write the following code, which colors the background of the cells in column A according to the index number of the color:

```
For ColIndex = 1 To 56

        Cells(ColIndex, 1).Interior.ColorIndex = ColIndex

Next
```

- By using the RGB code, for example:

```
ActiveCell.Interior.Color = RGB(200, 3, 8)
```

Remove modules

Right click on the module name and select **Remove module**.

You will be asked if you want to export the module before removing it, for backup use. If you choose to export it, the module will be saved in a ".bas" file.

Using the VBA Editor help

At any stage of the code writing you can use help in two ways:

1. From the **Help** menu:

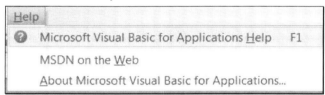

2. By writing a word in the VB editor and pressing F1

Immediate window

This window enables running code lines for examination purposes, without the need of running them from the code itself.

This option is available only while there is no code running (if the code was not activated, or if it reached a breakpoint)

Display the variable value

To display the variable value use the sign '**?**' (Question mark), and press **Enter** right after the command.

For example:

The above command will display the username as previously defined in the software.

In the same way, the following command:

Will show the row number of the active cell

Performing VBA commands

Type the command, without the question mark

The above command will enter the value 10 into cell A1

Note:

You can run only one command at a time

Another option of getting information in a window is by using the command **debug.print** inside the code.

This command does not affect the running of the code itself, and its purpose is to send information to the **Immediate** window (make sure the window is displayed...)

Keyboard Shortcuts

Key	Action
F1	Displays the **Help** window
F2	Displays the **Object Browser**
F3	Displays the next search result, after closing the **Search** window
Shift+F3	Displays the last search result, after closing the **Search** window
F4	Displays the **Properties** window
F5	Runs the entire procedure
F8	Runs the procedure step-by-step
F9	Adds and removes a breakpoint in the line where the cursor is located
Shift+F8	Step Over - While running a code in a'step-by-step'mode, which calls to another code, this keyboard shortcut enables the external code to be run as a whole, without entering into it ()
Ctrl+F8	Runs the code to the point where the cursor is
Ctrl+Shift+F8	Stops the code running
Ctrl+Shift+F9	Removes all breakpoints
Ctrl+C	Copy
Ctrl+X	Cut
Ctrl+V	Paste
Ctrl+Y	Cut an entire row
Ctrl+E	Displays the export code window
Ctrl+M	Displays the import code window

Key	Action
Ctrl+F	Displays the search window
Ctrl+G	Displays the immediate window
Ctrl+H	Displays the replace window
Ctrl+R	Displays the project explorer window
Ctrl+Z	Cancels the last action
Tab	Indents one line in
Shift+Tab	Indents one line out
Ctrl+Tab	Go to the next module
Ctrl+Break	Stop the code from running (especially effective when the code enters an infinite loop and we want to stop its execution)

Useful Codes

Cancel the copy and cut selection
After copy or cut command, the cell remains selected until the following command is executed:

```
Application.CutCopyMode = False
```

String reverse

```
ActiveCell = StrReverse(ActiveCell)
```

Range borders selection

```
Selection.Borders.LineStyle = xlSolid
```

Macro recording which adds borders to a range will result in a long macro, which adds a single borderline to each border – upper, lower, right, left, and middle borders (try it…). the above code will make the process shorter.

Sending a file by email

```
ActiveWorkbook.SendMail ("YourName@YourMail.com")
```

Making a "beep" sound

```
Beep
```

Displaying the 'open file' window

```
Application.Dialogs(xlDialogOpen).Show
```

Get Windows User Name:

```
MyUser = Environ("username")
```

Username retrieval, as this was entered into the Excel software

```
MyUser = Application.UserName
```

Creating a 'switch' for value changes

Some actions in Microsoft Excel have two possible states, for example – freezing a window: you can freeze a window or cancel the freezing. You can write two codes, one for freezing a window, and another one for unfreezing it. However, it is more elegant to write only one code, which checks the current value, and replaces it with the other one.

```
FrzPn = ActiveWindow.FreezePanes

ActiveWindow.FreezePanes = Not FrzPn
```

In the example above, we entered into a variable the command for freezing a window (which can get the value **True** or **False**).

Then we used the command NOT in order to change the value from True to False, and vice versa.

Prevention of user alert display

```
Application.DisplayAlerts = False
```

Explanation:

Many operations in Microsoft Excel display a message to the user.

For example, closing a workbook without saving the changes will display a dialog box asking whether to save your changes or not.

The following code cancels this dialog box.

Use it only if you want to prevent the user from having this choice.

You can change the command from False to True during the code, so you can have parts in the code that will not display alerts, and other parts that will.

Exercises

Exercise 1 – macro recording for conversion of formulas to values

1. Open the file **Sales 2007.xls** and select **January** sheet
2. Record a new macro (according to your version)
3. Give the macro the name My_Macro and save it in the current workbook
4. Record the following operations
   a. Select cell A1
   b. Select the entire data range (using the shortcut key Ctrl+*)
   c. Copy the entire range (in the 'Ribbon versions' – select the **Home** tab and in older versions select it from the **Edit** menu (or press the key combination Ctrl+C)
   d. Don't change the selected cell
   e. Right click and select the option **paste special**
   f. Select the **value** option
   g. Press Esc to cancel the copy state
   h. Press the shortcut key Ctrl+Home to go back to cell A1
   i. Press the button **Stop Recording**
5. Check the recording
   a. Select **February** sheet
   b. Check columns D and E – do the cells contain formulas?

   c. Press the button (in the 'Ribbon versions'), or select the menu **Tools → Macro → Macros** (in Excel 2003 version)
   d. In the displayed dialog box select My_Macro and press the **Run** button

e. Check whether the cells in the discount column contain values?

Check whether the macro is working properly on the **March** sheet as well?

Save the changes in a file. The saving includes the macro you have just recorded.

Exercise 2 – editing an existing macro

1. Open the file **Sale 2007.xls**
2. Open the macro editor: in the 'Ribbon versions' press the button in the **Developer** tab, and in older versions select from the menu **Tools → Macro → Macros**
3. Select the **Edit** button
4. Now you can see the code as it was written while being recorded
5. Place the cursor before the **End Sub** line
6. Add the following code lines:

```
Range("A1").Select

Range(Selection, Selection.End(xlToRight)).Select

Selection.Interior.Color = vbYellow

Selection.Font.Bold = True

Range("A1").Select

Selection.CurrentRegion.Select

Selection.Borders.LineStyle = xlSolid

Range("a1").Select

MsgBox ("Congratulations, you have just written your first code")
```

7. Close the VBA editor and go back to the Excel file
8. Go to the **April** sheet
9. Run the macro My_Macro on the **April** sheet
10. Click the message which appears at the end of the running code

Did your typed additions take place?

Did you get a congratulations message?

If so, you just wrote your first real code!

Exercise 3 – writing code for data ranges
1. Open the file **ranges.xls** in sheet 1
2. Open the VBA editor and create a new module
3. Add a new macro and name it My_Ranges
4. Write a code that performs the following actions:
   a. Select cell A1
   b. Select the data set range in column A (from cell A1 to the last cell with data in the column)
   c. Color the range in blue
   d. Select all cells with data in the range
   e. Align the cells content to the center
   f. Go to the cell below the last data cell in column A
   g. Add the text **"new row"**
   h. Go to the next cell in the row (in column B) and color it in yellow
   i. Go to cell A1
5. Run the code step by step and check if it works properly on the table in sheet 2 as well

Exercise 4 – writing a code using 'With' structure
In a new Excel file write a code that performs the following actions:

1. Select a range that begins with the cell A1, but its size is unknown
2. On the selected range we will perform the following actions using 'With' structure
   a. Centralize the text
   b. Color the cells in red
   c. Color the text in yellow
   d. Change the font size to 11
   e. Set border lines to the table cells
   f. Enter the value 1234 in each table cell

Note,

The code should work properly for every table range we will run it on. At the end of the code cell A1 will remain selected

Exercise 5 - Loops

In this exercise you will create the colors board

Remember, each color in Excel has a numeric value (the number of the yellow color is 6, for example, and we call it by the command colorindex=6)

1. Write the colors numbers (from 1 to 56) in column A
2. Color the font in each cell in column A by its index number (for example - the font of the cell with the number 6 will be colored in yellow)
3. The adjacent cell in column B will be colored by using the index color number of column A

Exercise 6 – loops combine in an IF command

1. Write a work plan for checking a range of cells
   a. Cells which contain a positive even number will be colored in yellow

b. Cells which contain a positive odd number will be colored in blue

c. Cells which contain a non-integer number will be colored in red

d. Cells which contain a negative number will be colored in green (even if they were previously colored in a different color)